Help for Pain and Suffering

Stories and Reflections

Russell M. Abata, C.SS.R., S.T.D.

LIGUORI
PUBLICATIONS

One Liguori Drive
Liguori, Missouri 63057-9999
(314) 464-2500

Imprimi Potest:
James Shea, C.SS.R.
Provincial, St. Louis Province
The Redemptorists

Imprimatur:
Monsignor Maurice F. Byrne
Vice Chancellor, Archdiocese of St. Louis

ISBN 0-89243-349-3
Library of Congress Catalog Card Number: 91-72203

Cover design by Chris Sharp

Contents

Introduction

The message read, "Your brother is in a lot of pain. He is dying of cancer. It would be good if you went to see him." Putting the note down, I gazed out the window.

Of course I would go. The full schedule of activities that had seemed so important moments ago now faded into the background. All I had to do was rearrange my plans enough to get away for a few days.

But I was afraid. When I got there, what would I say? This was my brother. I wouldn't be able to approach his suffering from the safe distance of my intellect. His pain and fear would become mine. Was I ready for that?

As a priest I could remind my brother of the things he knew very well — that God loved him and would help him somehow. He knew these things, but perhaps the pain had pushed them aside. As a professional counselor I could listen to him and try to understand what he was experiencing. (But can a person ever understand another's pain?) I could even offer some words of advice, words I had used with other people. But this was different — this was my brother.

I also knew that my presence itself, my being there, would tell him how much I love him.

But I wasn't confident I could reassure my brother "everything would work out all right." What does that phrase mean anyway? I knew that a person's words and presence can be helpful, but how helpful to someone who was in deep pain, to someone who was dying of cancer? I did not know.

My visit went by very quickly. As I left my brother said, "Just say good-bye, nothing more." Although I was churned up inside, I did as he had said. I walked away. On the way to the airport, I wondered if I had helped in any way. I wasn't sure. Even so, I was glad I had come. More importantly, he was glad I had come.

Back in Manhattan, after I had a chance to reflect over the situation, I felt there was so much more I could have said. Because my brother's cancer was so advanced, I don't think I'll ever have the opportunity. But maybe I can share it with you. Maybe my words will mean something to you or to other people. I hope so.

If this booklet helps someone even in a small way, it will be worth the effort.

Dear Reader, throughout this booklet I want to talk to you as directly as I can. Pain and suffering are very personal matters. A book about these topics should also be as personal as we can make it. That is why at times I have put into words what I felt might be your responses to the ideas presented. In any given case you might put it a different way, but if it touches on what you *feel,* then I think it will be helpful. If you compose your own response in those places or in answering the end-of-chapter questions, all the better.

The purpose of this booklet is to help you understand what your suffering is all about. Maybe, then, just maybe, it will be a little easier to bear. Meanwhile, be assured that my heart goes out to you — much like it goes out to my brother. I want to say thank you for allowing me to share these thoughts with you.

Russell Abata, C.SS.R.

1

Looking for Help

The beginning of any book is difficult. But I know where to begin this one. If you are experiencing pain right now, then there's one thing on your mind, there's one thing occupying your full attention. Relief. How can you find relief from your pain?

Since this is your biggest concern, it's where I want to start. So the first question is: can this book provide any relief?

Yes, I believe it can.

So, whether you believe this or not (and I don't blame you for being skeptical), let's begin.

Seeking Help

Your first impulse when you are in trouble is to seek help. If it's a medical problem, you look for a doctor. If it's a financial problem, you turn to a friend or relative. If it's a decision problem, you seek a trusted person or a counselor. As soon as there is a glimmer of hope that help might be coming, you begin to feel relieved. You still have your problem, but you feel better.

But what if you have no place to turn for help, what then?

This might be where you find yourself right now. You have turned to the skilled professionals, the doctors and counselors; you have reached out to your friends who wanted to help but were unable; you have even pleaded with God; yet you are still suffering. No wonder you feel crushed under your burden. No wonder you feel so alone.

Where can you find help?

Try God Again

I would suggest that you try God again. This time work with God. As discouraged and tired as you are, try to understand what is happening. Since it appears God is not helping you, ask yourself why. You will probably come up with the wrong reasons, but at least they will be out on the table. You might be thinking things like this:

- *God is punishing me because of the things I have done.*
- *God is not fair. He is helping those he loves more.*
- *God doesn't care about me. I'm not worth caring about.*

Maybe you have no reasons. Maybe your mind is too exhausted to come up with reasons. Everything is turned off inside of you, except pain and fear. You don't know what to think or feel.

It's precisely because of how you feel that you need the reassurance of God's help. The pit you are in is so deep and so dark you need the best help possible to get out of it. If you can convince yourself that God is helping you, you will have hope. You will feel better.

But how can I convince myself God is helping me when I see no evidence that he is? I feel he has let me down. I used to go to him, and I felt he helped me, but not lately. I don't want to be let down anymore. It's too painful. So I don't think I can go back to God. What would I do or say that I haven't already done or said? At best, I'm confused about God. At worst, I'm deeply disappointed and bitter about him.

Realize Who God Is

If you feel this way, maybe your first step in returning to God is to realize who God is. God is God. There will be times when you will not understand what he is doing. But you can be sure of one thing. Whether you realize it or not, God is all-knowing and all-loving. His special plan for you is filled with wisdom and love.

Can you rise above your pain enough to consider this special loving plan God has for you?

God has a special loving plan for me? I don't accept that. If God is so loving, why can't he find a way to help me? If I knew how to free a loved one from pain, I would do it in an instant. So I don't see how talking about God's loving plan is going to help. If anything, it will make me more angry and bitter.

I can appreciate how you feel, but can you see that your suffering might be serving a purpose above your present understanding? God knows the purpose. Some day you will know it too. In the meantime, can you try to trust God?

When Job of the Old Testament realized how superior God was to himself, it helped him immensely. He had lived a good life, so why was he suffering? Why was God not helping him? Job couldn't find any answers at first, but then he remembered God was far greater than he was and must know what he was doing. Once Job really realized that, he humbled himself and trusted God. A weight lifted off his back and he felt better immediately.

Can you take this first step of accepting that God has reasons for allowing you to suffer? And that these reasons, despite appearances, are loving. It will make you feel better if you can accept this. It will help you take the next step of trying to find out those reasons.

Two Ways Out

God has given you two ways out of your dungeon of pain and suffering.

One way is by looking at how Jesus used his sufferings. Our Savior had a mission to accomplish that involved him in a great amount of suffering. How did he handle his pain? How does he want you to handle yours? Jesus knows the best way for handling pain. It will profit you to discover and follow his way.

The second way is by examining how pain works. When you push aside how terrible you feel and take a good look, you see that pain happens when something is broken or deficient or mal-functioning within yourself. This applies to your whole self — body and soul. If your feelings are deprived for a long time or are not as developed as they should be, they cry out with pain. A person cannot cope with adult responsibilities with only a child's develop-ment. The strain and pain become overwhelming.

So you have two ways to bring yourself safely through your sufferings. One way is taught by Jesus, the other you can figure out yourself. Both are helpful. Jesus gives you God's viewpoint. Your reasoning powers give you a common-sense view of things. In the next two chapters, we will consider both at length. Before we do that, let me tell you what happened when a good man came face to face with suffering.

* * *

Joe was twenty-eight when something happened that changed his life. He encountered the suffering Jesus in a fellow human being. This took place during his last year of internship in a big hospital in New York City.

Joe was only three when his father died, leaving his mother with ten children. He grew up in a tough neighborhood. The Depression was in full swing. His Italian mother wore black most of his childhood. Not knowing where to turn for guidance, Joe's thoughts often turned to his father in heaven. Which one? His human father or his heavenly Father? More often than not, he turned to his heavenly Father. In some ways he was the only father Joe knew. He was too young when his father died to know him.

Somehow the family survived. Joe was intense in everything he did. He worked and studied with a passion. At first he thought he would be a priest, but he convinced himself that being a dedicated doctor would also be a life where he could do much good. He graduated from medical school with honors.

Every day as an intern Joe saw suffering of every kind. It bothered him, but he managed to handle his doubts about the basic goodness of life. He was able to do this until the day he stood before a little child who had been beaten to death by his drunk parents. As he looked at that poor little bruised body, he saw more than the child. He saw the crumpled, broken body of the innocent Jesus. For the first time, the crucifix became real and ugly.

Joe did what he had to and left the room. His eyes were brimming with tears. His face was white. Spasms gripped his insides. He cried bitterly, "My God, my God, why did you forsake your Son? Why did you forsake this child? Will I ever understand you? I hope so. I'm going to need your help constantly if I'm going to be a good doctor."

Joe never missed daily Mass.

* * *

1. Since your serious encounter with suffering, have you become bitter about life? Do you feel helpless?
2. Have you stopped believing that God will help you overcome what you are suffering?
3. What is your picture of God? Do you have trouble getting a picture of God as loving and wise?
4. Do you have any ideas why the Father of Jesus allowed him to suffer?
5. What is the real purpose of pain?

2

Going to Jesus for Help

As you start this chapter some questions might be troubling you. If you have not taken Jesus seriously for a long time, how can you approach him for help now? You might be thinking how you would feel if someone you hardly knew was driven by desperation to ask you for money. Would you help him or her?

Forget your worries. Jesus will welcome you no matter who you are or what you've done. He never turned away anyone who came to him. He says, "Come to me, all you who labor and are burdened, and I will give you rest" (Matthew 11:28).

But how will he give me rest?

He will do so in three ways.

He will give rest to your mind by answering the doubts suffering has stirred up about God, about God's goodness and his love. He will show you God's purpose for allowing suffering and his plan for dealing with it.

He will give rest to your feelings of desperation and loneliness by reassuring you of his presence and help throughout your ordeal.

He will give rest to your body by eliminating your pain or helping you bear it.

Jesus and You

In a few words Jesus will help you by working with you. To encourage you, Jesus uses a homespun example. He asks you to think how the farmer joins animals by way of a yoke so they can pull a plow or wagon together: "Take my yoke upon you and learn from me, for I am meek and humble of heart; and you will find rest for yourselves" (Matthew 11:29).

This is Jesus' invitation. He is willing to go into a partnership with you to help you through your suffering. Will you accept his invitation?

I'm not sure I can. Jesus says we will be harnessed together. I don't want to sound ungrateful, but that's not what I am looking for. I don't want Jesus to work with me. I want him to take away my pain. Instead of making me feel better, all this talk is making me feel worse.

Do not give up and run away. Jesus is not asking you to do what is beyond you. Working with him, you will find the strength to carry your burden. He indicates this when he says, "For my yoke is easy, and my burden light" (Matthew 11:30).

The helplessness of your suffering can teach you how much your life depends on God. Without God, you would not exist. Without his help, you are helpless. Recognizing this is what meekness and humility are all about. Jesus himself learned new dimensions of meekness and humility from his suffering. He wants you to learn the same.

If you are willing to accept Jesus' invitation, tell him, "Jesus, I accept your help. I will join myself to you. We will do what we have to do together."

All right, I'm not sure of myself, but I'll try to accept Jesus' offer of help. What happens next?

Take a moment to let the full meaning of what you are accepting sink in. You are accepting Jesus' working with you, shoulder to shoulder. You are accepting his active presence in your life. It means Jesus is with you. You are no longer alone in your suffering. What a tremendous consolation that can be.

Jesus Within You

Not only is Jesus with you, he is within you. His words are "Whoever loves me will keep my word, and my Father will love him, and we will come to him and make our dwelling with him" (John 14:23).

I've heard this before. I had difficulty trying to understand it then; I have greater difficulty with it now. Jesus is not actually present in me as a person, is he?

Yes, he is. And the Father and the Holy Spirit are dwelling within you also. It takes an act of faith to believe that, especially when your sufferings are wearing you down. Whether you feel it or not, it's the gospel truth. It can be a great consolation. That awareness can be like the net for the acrobat. Knowing the net is there, the high-wire performer will do things he or she wouldn't do without it. Knowing that God is within you means you can do things you could not do alone.

Your suffering can be an opportunity to trust God. When things are going well, it's not too difficult to trust him. That is what the tempter said in the Book of Job: "Is it for nothing that Job is God-fearing? Have you not surrounded him and his family and all that he has with your protection?...But now put forth your hand and touch anything that he has, and surely he will blaspheme you to your face" (Job 1:9-10, 11). Even after everything was taken from Job, he did not turn against God. Will you? This doesn't mean that you can't cry out to God for what is happening to you. That's all right, but after you have let out your fear and anger, if you can tell God you still trust him, then that trust is more precious than fire-tried gold.

Of itself, suffering is not good. You should do what you can to get rid of it. But as a challenge of trust, it can be precious. It is like the sacrifices one makes to demonstrate one's love for another person. The sacrifices themselves are not wanted; the love is. It is the love that makes the sacrifices acceptable and precious.

Jesus and Suffering

It's time to consider God's ideas about suffering. We will rely on Jesus and his teaching for our instruction.

If we look at Jesus' sufferings, we see that they happen to him as he carries out his mission. His favorite theme, "I am the good shepherd," gives us valuable information about both his mission and his sufferings. (See John 10:1-21.)

His mission as a good shepherd is to lead his sheep to the nourishing pastures of love. He knows our hearts will not be filled or at rest without a complete love. So he teaches us about his Father and his Father's kingdom. He urges us to love everyone. He is very clear about loving ourselves above material things.

His sufferings come from the opposition he met as he tried to carry out his mission of teaching love and doing good. The hypocritical leaders of his day opposed him. His honesty and humility were too much for them. Although it would mean suffering, Jesus would not back down. Eventually, they would kill him. He accepted this torture and cruel death to give us an example of not giving up when we meet difficulties in doing good.

Are you saying that Jesus' death was not something planned by the Father to redeem or pay the price of sin? I thought his death was an essential part of the plan. Are you saying it was not?

The Father's Plan

The Father's plan for Jesus was to teach love. The Father wanted Jesus' obedience, trust, and love — not his death. As the psalmist says, "For you are not pleased with sacrifices; / should I offer a holocaust, you would not accept it. / My sacrifice, O God, is a contrite spirit; / a heart contrite and humbled, O God, you will not spurn" (Psalm 51:18-19). It was Jesus' willingness to die rather than disobey or show lack of trust that was pleasing to the Father. His acceptance of his death showed the depth of his love. It was the high point of his teaching on love. "No one has greater love than this, to lay down one's life for one's friends" (John 15:13).

If what you are saying is true, it throws a different light on suffering. All along I thought the Father was cruel in wanting his Son's death. You are showing me that this is not the case. If it's not the case for Jesus, maybe the same holds true for me. The Father doesn't want me to suffer. He wants my obedience, trust, and love. Is that right?

Yes, that's correct.

Discipline

As we examine Jesus' approach to suffering in the gospels, we hear the echo of his teaching in other New Testament writings.

The Letter to the Hebrews says, "Endure your trials as 'discipline'; God treats you as sons. For what 'son' is there whom his father does not discipline?…Besides this, we have had our earthly fathers to discipline us, and we respected them. Should we not [then] submit all the more to the Father of spirits and live? They disciplined us for a short time as seemed right to them, but he does so for our benefit, in order that we may share his holiness. At the time, all discipline seems a cause not for joy but for pain, yet later it brings the peaceful fruit of righteousness to those who are trained by it. So strengthen your drooping hands and your weak knees" (12:7-12).

As you listen to these comments that trials and suffering are a discipline from God, you might wonder, "Does the author of this inspired New Testament Letter mean that discipline is a punishment from God?"

No, not quite. In those days the word *discipline* meant a learning experience. Some universities still use it in this sense. They speak of the discipline of medicine or law. It's in this sense that a student is called a disciple — someone who learns. In this sense suffering can teach us so much. A degree from the school of hard knocks is worth more than an academic degree from the most prestigious university.

Saint Paul and Suffering

Saint Paul views suffering in much the same way. He sees it as earning the rewards of self-sufficiency and true virtue in this life and immense joy and glory in eternal life.

He says, "...I have learned, in whatever situation I find myself, to be self-sufficient....I have learned the secret of being well fed and of going hungry, of living in abundance and of being in need. I have the strength for everything through him who empowers me" (Philippians 4:11-13).

He speaks about true virtue, "Not only that, but we even boast of our afflictions, knowing that affliction produces endurance, and endurance, proven character, and proven character, hope" (Romans 5:3-4).

Saint Paul continues: "Therefore, we are not discouraged; rather, although our outer self is wasting away, our inner self is being renewed day by day. For this momentary light affliction is producing for us an eternal weight of glory beyond all comparison" (2 Corinthians 4:16-17). And in the Letter to the Romans he adds: "I consider that the sufferings of this present time are as nothing compared with the glory to be revealed for us" (8:18).

But is it correct to say that the sufferings earn the reward?

No, not quite. It is really love that counts. "So faith, hope, love remain, these three; but the greatest of these is love" (1 Corinthians 13:13). Saint Paul made that clear with these words: "If I give away everything I own, and if I hand my body over so that I may boast but do not have love, I gain nothing" (1 Corinthians 13:3).

Of course, for Saint Paul and the other sacred writers, the main reason for accepting suffering is that it enables us to be like Jesus in every possible way.

The Power of Faith

Another word for this approach to life is faith. Again and again Jesus insists on faith. He says that if you have the right kind of faith, you can move mountains. "Amen, I say to you, if you have faith the size of a mustard seed, you will say to this mountain, 'Move from here to there,' and it will move" (Matthew 17:20). Faith is extremely powerful. It can even move God to work a miracle in your favor. A strong faith can convince God to set aside the ordinary laws of nature and actually work a miracle.

What do you mean? Are you saying there is a price tag on miracles? I thought Jesus said we could call his Father, our Father. Would a good father place a condition on helping his son or daughter? Isn't need, desperate need, enough reason to help a child?

Yes, Jesus' Father is our Father, and he is a good Father who is concerned about our needs. Because he is concerned, he has given us a world that is well stocked with food, medicine, and human intelligence to solve our problems. As God's sons and daughters, everyone has a right to these resources. The primary consideration in distributing them should be need. Other considerations of intelligence, beauty, or special talents should be secondary. These natural resources should be sufficient to handle our problems.

If these resources are not enough, you can go directly to God for special help. Jesus acknowledges this when he says, "Ask and it will be given to you; seek and you will find; knock and the door will be opened to you" (Matthew 7:7).

But I have asked, sought, and knocked — and nothing has happened. Why hasn't it? Do I have the wrong kind of faith? Isn't it strong enough?

A strong faith is certainly needed — and also perseverance in asking. God wants you to continue to ask to strengthen your faith. Trees shaken by the wind sink the deepest roots. Faith does the same. To continue to believe when you see no results is the kind of belief that works miracles. As you see in the following story, it was what worked the miracle for the Canaanite woman.

Leaving God Speechless

"A Canaanite woman of that district came and called out, 'Have pity on me, Lord, Son of David! My daughter is tormented by a demon.' But he did not say a word in answer to her. His disciples came and asked him, 'Send her away, for she keeps calling out after us.' He said in reply, 'I was sent only to the lost sheep of the house of Israel.' But the woman came and did him homage, saying, 'Lord, help me.' He said in reply, 'It is not right to take the food of the children and throw it to the dogs.' She said, 'Please, Lord, for even the dogs eat the scraps that fall from the table of their masters.' Then Jesus said to her in reply, 'O woman, great is your faith! Let it be done for you as you wish.' And her daughter was healed from that hour" (Matthew 15:22-28).

At the beginning of this story, Jesus seemed to be paying no attention to the woman's pleading for help. This was most strange. She wasn't asking for herself. She was begging Jesus to help her daughter. What was wrong? So many times Jesus had embraced little children and said how precious they were. This time he treats the mother and child as if they were not there. Does that sound familiar? How many times have you cried out to God and he seemed to be ignoring you?

Did this silent treatment stop the woman? No, she kept after Jesus. Finally, the disciples begged Jesus to get rid of her. He wouldn't do that. He hadn't finished his encounter with her. But Jesus told his disciples he could not do anything for her because she was a stranger.

Still the woman would not give up. She kept after him, begging for help.

Then Jesus insulted her. He called her and her people dogs. He said he cannot give the food of the children to the dogs.

The woman absorbed the rebuff and replied that sometimes the leftover crumbs are given to the dogs, especially to the sick, helpless puppies.

Jesus listened. He was speechless. She had won over his heart. She was rewarded with a miracle for her daughter.

The same kind of faith works miracles today.

Are you saying I have to have the kind of faith that leaves God speechless before I can obtain his special help? Forget it. I'm not capable of such faith. I'm having difficulty holding on to a basic belief, a belief that God is good and that he cares about me. I could never have a faith as strong as that woman.

A Mustard Seed

But you can have such a faith. Even if your faith is as tiny as a mustard seed, it can grow. You can help it grow. As badly as you feel, try not to lose heart. Try to hold on so your faith can sink its roots deep into your being. If you feel yourself doubting, do like the father of the sick boy who cried out to Jesus with tears, "I do believe, help my unbelief!" (Mark 9:24).

I don't know. This kind of faith has more to it than I thought. I thought believing was principally an intellectual thing. Now I'm seeing that it's much more. It's not only acknowledging that God exists, it's accepting the whole picture. It's accepting God as God, regardless of what he does.

Yes, that's the kind of faith that's needed. If you could acquire it, it would make you resemble Jesus in his supreme act of faith in the Garden of Gethsemane. Like any other human, our Savior wanted no part of the cup of suffering. He begged his Father, "My Father, if it is possible, let this cup pass from me." The words were hardly out of his mouth when his faith took hold of him and he abandoned himself into his Father's hands. "My Father, if it is not possible that this cup pass without my drinking it, your will be done!" (See Matthew 26:36-46.) And if your faith is like Jesus', it will be able to pull you through your agony of suffering.

Remember, the Father's answer to suffering is Jesus. Accept him, love him, copy him, trust him, and believe in him without doubts or questions. He says of himself, "I came into the world as light, so that everyone who believes in me might not remain in darkness" (John 12:46). Hold on to Jesus and do not let him go. Tell him how difficult it is for you to hold on. Ask him for help.

In the following story Katherine experiences her Gethsemane.

* * *

Katherine was in her sixties when life became more than she could bear. The final blow came when her son died from AIDS. The shock was more than she could handle. She had to be hospitalized for three months.

Before the death of her son, she would say that having learned to deal with her husband's debilitating sickness after her fourth child was born, she could handle anything. But it was not so. Seeing her Joey in the casket was too much. All her fears and frustrations broke loose. She could not control them; they controlled her. Although a devout person from her youth, she gave up on God. He was nowhere in sight. Maybe he was too busy helping others. He certainly wasn't helping her.

Once the hospital chaplain saw her name and religion on the newcomer's list, he paid her a visit. Because she was so distraught, he only said hello, stayed a few moments, and left. Although he had never studied psychology, he knew enough about pain not to argue with it. He came every day and stood off to the side and looked at her with understanding eyes.

At first Katherine resented the priest's visits, but she was too refined to say or show her resentment. Slowly, she began to look forward to them, especially to look into his eyes. They were so revealing of his caring.

After two weeks of being strongly medicated, she cried and shook less. Then she even managed a "Good morning, Father. Thanks for coming." Unfortunately or fortunately, she started to cry again. With a pleading, almost little girl's voice, she begged, "Father, why is God doing this to me? I haven't done anything really wrong. Why my little Joey? With his father so sick, he became attached to me. We were so close." She became hysterical.

The priest did not say a word. He was only going to look at her, but that left too great a distance between them. He automatically took her hand and was pleasantly surprised at how tightly she held on. A bridge had formed between them. He stayed a few moments and left.

The next day when he returned, he saw a spark of light in her eyes that was not there before. "Is it all right if I call you Katherine?" he asked in a nonassuming way. She nodded approval.

"Katherine, do you pray?"

"I used to, Father, but I have not done so for a while. I don't think God loves me. I've prayed and prayed for my family, but it hasn't done any good. My husband is an invalid. My son is dead. I'm in here like a vegetable. I feel like a piece of junk they had to cart away. If you were in my situation, Father, would you believe God loves you?"

"Katherine," the priest said softly, "I'm a late vocation. I fed, clothed, and took care of my invalid wife for twenty years. In the beginning it was awful; after a while it was not so bad. In the end it was a joy. We became so close that after she died I could never love another woman the same way. That is when I decided to apply for entrance into the priesthood. Katherine, I do not know the mind of God very well, but I believe he wants our good. I can't say any more than that. I see you are a good woman. You will find your way back to belief. Take your time. Maybe this time it will be more as a woman than as a child. If you ever want to talk or to receive

Jesus in holy Communion, please let me know. It will be my privilege to bring him to you."

* * *

1. Do you understand the offer of help Jesus extends to those who are heavily burdened? What does it mean when the Bible says he will help you carry your burdens? In your weakened condition, how much of your cross can you carry?
2. Do you have difficulty realizing that Jesus is not only with you but also within you? How can you help yourself realize this?
3. Of itself, is suffering something good? Can it lead to something good? What?
4. What is discipline? How is suffering a discipline?
5. What works miracles?
6. What is God's answer to suffering?

3

Consulting Nature for Understanding

In the last chapter you went to Jesus to find God's views on suffering. In this chapter you will consult your own reason to see what it can tell you about pain and suffering.

Clearly, pain is keeping you from doing many things you would like to do. To put it mildly, it has been a real hindrance to your enjoyment of life. No wonder you would like to be free of it. Even so, have you ever thought of pain as providing a service for you, as being helpful?

What are you talking about? I'm beside myself with pain and you want me to see it as providing a service, as being helpful. Do you really understand what I'm going through?

Yes, I understand and sympathize with you, but I don't think it's wise to dismiss what your reason tells you about pain. Some of what it says might even help you get rid of or at least cope with your pain. It's worth listening to.

Nature's Plan

This is the question we should ask: how does pain fit into nature's plan?

Pain helps you survive. It warns you about things that are harmful and it alerts you when things need correcting. An example would be a toothache. It tells you about the presence of a cavity or an abscess. If you don't deal with the problem now, you will experience further damage and more pain later. That's the way nature works. It wants you to survive. It has equipped you with a variety of system checks to do this. When parts of you are not well or not working well, they send out pain signals so other parts can come to the rescue.

What are you saying? I've been in pain for a long time. Why haven't other parts of me come to the rescue?

They have. It takes time for nature to heal what is broken or to destroy what is attacking you.

Time. I know people who have been sick all their lives. What happened to nature's rescue plan for them?

Their rescue plan might be to reach for a higher level. They might have to make up for their physical weakness by looking inside themselves for emotional or spiritual strength.

What do you mean? What higher strength can people have when they are being destroyed by pain?

Hidden Powers

People have powers inside of them they might not know they have. All of us have known individuals who have overcome tremendous odds, who have risen above great suffering or incapacitating physical handicaps to lead extraordinary lives. Their pains or the limitations of their illnesses have somehow challenged them to live their lives on a higher, more rewarding plane. Somehow they have managed to reach inside themselves and release powers that they did not know they had.

Are you trying to tell me that I have powers within me that I'm not aware of?

Yes, that's what I'm saying. Most people don't realize their coping powers. It's probably because they haven't been taught by word or example where to find or how to release these powers. A good example is constructive anger. Let me show you how the process works.

When you are afraid, your first reaction is to deny the fear itself. You tell yourself that you are not afraid. This is probably what you did when you first experienced pain. "Oh, it's nothing. It will go away," you said. It did not go away.

Next you tried to distract yourself from it by thinking of other things or simply by not thinking. If this didn't work, you ran to someone who might be able to help you. You went to a doctor or you called out to God. If that didn't take care of the problem, you didn't know what to do. Some people break down at this point. They fall into despair. Some turn to anger, a very destructive anger. They want to destroy what is hurting them. If that doesn't work, they try to destroy things or people who are not helping them. At times, in their frustration, they try to destroy even those who are trying to help them but are not succeeding very well.

Constructive Anger

Besides destructive anger there is a more valuable type of anger that can be called upon. It is a constructive anger. It gives you the power to stand and fight if that's what is called for. If fighting is not helpful, this power helps you to stand and hold your ground. You refuse to give up, and you refuse to waste the experience by going overboard feeling sorry for yourself. You are determined to learn what you can from what is happening.

What do you mean? What can a person learn from suffering? I'll tell you what I've learned so far. That pain is terrible. That suffering can be a degrading experience. That a person can become bitter toward God for allowing this to happen.

Yes, many have learned this from their suffering, but it's not the only lesson that can be learned. One of the greatest lessons you can learn is the truth about your mortality and your total dependence on God for everything. If you can take that approach, then you can say with Saint Paul, "I will rather boast most gladly of my weaknesses, in order that the power of Christ may dwell with me. Therefore, I am content with weaknesses, insults, hardships, persecutions, and constraints, for the sake of Christ; for when I am weak, then I am strong" (2 Corinthians 12:9-10).

Do I have this right? Are you saying that anger, constructive anger, can help me when I am deep into suffering? How?

Yes. First, if you are delaying out of fear to have a treatment that can help your condition, constructive anger strengthens your determination to do it.

Second, if you are frightened because nothing can be done about your physical condition, constructive anger can help you not to be consumed or destroyed by your fear. It converts itself into courage. As well as you can, as long as you have life, you will value your life as a gift of God.

Third, if your death is approaching, it will give you the courage to accept it as best you can. You will be frightened, even terrified, but deep inside you will find the power to accept it.

It sounds like this constructive anger is very good. But all I have is pain, fear, and weakness. How do I find this constructive anger I'm supposed to have?

You find it by doing it. You tell yourself, "I'm afraid and in pain, but I refuse to be overcome by them. I don't know how, but somehow I'll hold on." Repeat these or similar words as often as you can.

In the beginning these words seem meaningless, useless. But they are not. Slowly, your anger begins to take hold and becomes a kind of courage. Slowly your courage becomes a quiet confidence. It helps you to believe in the quality of life God put into nature.

Let's see if nature has any other helps.

Your Deeper Mind

Besides constructive anger, nature has given you your deeper powers of reason to help you. To appreciate this you have to realize that your mind has different depths to it. You have a surface mind and a deeper one that can get under things to understand your pain, fear, and weakness better.

Your surface mind is often controlled by your feelings. Your feelings put your mind to work to figure out ways to get pleasure and avoid pain. If the pain is unavoidable, they get your mind to seek ways to cut down on it. Obviously, this can be helpful.

When it comes to really deep suffering, this surface mind is of little or no help. If it's under the control of your feelings, it doesn't know how to avoid the pain you are suffering. It is more of a burden than a help.

But it's not this way with your deeper mind. Your deeper mind is more concerned over what is happening than with the pain you are experiencing. It is asking: what is the pain trying to say? Is there something that is physically, emotionally, or spiritually wrong?

Wait a minute. What are you talking about? I think I know what you mean by my surface mind. What I don't understand is this deeper mind.

Looking Beyond the Pain

Your deeper mind is functioning when you can see things that are not immediately obvious. Pain is pain. Even a child understands that. You feel it and want to get rid of it. This is the immediate reaction of your surface mind. Your deeper mind can look beyond the pain. Besides probing what is wrong and needs correcting, it asks how this experience will help you become a better person. Can you be patient with yourself? Can you keep from being swallowed by your fears? Can you find an inner strength to cope with what is happening?

Do you mean to tell me that people who are suffering terribly can ask and answer questions like these?

Yes, they can, if they are using their deeper mind.

I don't believe it. I'm a simple person. With suffering, I want out. That's all there is to it.

I understand how you feel. A time of pain is no time to talk about your deeper mind, or is it? When would most take time to take a better look at living? It is only when they are on their backs that they look up to see if there is more to life than they have seen.

Your deeper mind says there is. As with constructive anger, you have to slow down and allow it to function. If you cannot do this alone, it is worth your efforts to seek help. You don't want to miss out on this valuable help nature has given you.

To repeat, nature uses pain to tell you that something is wrong. This holds true whether the pain is physical, emotional, or spiritual. It's up to you or to someone professional to find out what is wrong. With the proper help it is hoped that the defect can be discovered and corrected.

If the defect cannot be remedied, then nature supplies you with constructive anger and the use of your deeper mind to find ways to cope with the defect and the pain it is causing.

And now a story about a man who took a good look at himself.

* * *

For the past thirty years William has lived with the horrors of asthma. He would gasp for air as if he were drowning. His wheezing would alert everyone with apprehension. Fortunately, the specialist his parents consulted was able to prescribe medication that helped him breathe normally.

To his family, others, and himself, William's condition was seen as something physical. His suffering was telling him that something was not working correctly in the chest area of his body. Regardless of what was triggering it — atmospheric conditions or something else — it was all physical.

29

After some serious attacks when he could not get his breath and thought he would die, William became desperate with fear. He told some close friends how he felt. They advised him, "Go for some counseling. Even if your condition is physical, it is having psychological effects on you."

William took their advice and went to a priest-counselor whom a friend recommended.

The first weeks of his counseling were a running account about his asthmatic attacks and fears. He spoke of how furious he was with God for not helping him to find relief.

The priest listened reassuringly and nodded in agreement with how difficult it must be to live with such a condition. He also said that his feelings against God were understandable.

One day, at the end of a session, the priest said, "William, I am sure your worry about your condition has triggered panic, anger, and depression in you. Did you ever stop to think that maybe it is the other way around? Maybe you have a panic and anger that is triggering your asthma attacks? Today, although you have talked about your mother's death and the panic it has caused you, you have not used your inhaler once. Isn't it possible that your asthma is more a lack of emotional expression and emotional development than a physical condition?"

William agreed it was possible.

As the months of counseling continued, it became more and more obvious to the counselor and to William that his attacks were definitely connected to his emotions. He was still a little boy who felt a desperate need for his mother. He would pretend she was around, somewhere. Any time he was in trouble and realized she wasn't, he would panic, tighten up in his chest, and have an attack. He could hardly breathe.

Accepting the supposition that this lack of emotional development could be a serious contributor to his attacks, the counselor and William shifted their attention from his asthma to his need to correct and complete the emotional level of his personality.

"William," the priest said one day, "can you see that your suffering is not some kind of unfair punishment and that God has not forgotten you? Rather, God wants you to take a good look at your suffering to see what needs to be done to complete yourself as a whole person."

Moved by an enormous respect for the wisdom and patience of his counselor, William could not find any better words to say than "Thank you, Father."

* * *

1. How do you look on pain, as a help or a hindrance?
2. Do you know anyone with a serious handicap who has reached down inside to find strengths that most do not have?
3. What is constructive anger? How can it help you? How do you get in touch with it?
4. Is your thinking always on the surface level or are you capable of deeper thinking? Are you able to look beyond pain to see what it is trying to tell you?

4

Bringing the
Teachings Together

Having looked at suffering from the viewpoints of Jesus and nature — revelation and your own reason — we want to see if and how they fit together.

Since Jesus and nature both speak the truth, they cannot oppose each other. They must support each other. Actually, together they give us a better picture than they would individually.

We saw that Jesus approaches suffering by offering you a helping hand. By his example of a faith-filled, hope-filled, and love-filled obedience in doing his Father's will, Jesus shows you how to make your life and suffering profitable. He promises to be with you as you face the hardships of life. If your faith is strong, he will either work a miracle and take away what you are suffering, or he will give you the strength and courage to bear it.

So, in great part, Jesus has a practical approach to suffering. He emphasizes the assurance of his help. You don't have to live your life or carry your burdens alone. He will do his part, if you let him, and if you do your part. What is your part? Besides working on your faith and trust in God, you have to use the tools God has placed in your nature for cases of emergencies. These are your constructive anger and the use of your deeper mind.

Faith and Your Deeper Mind

As the Scripture says, God's ways of acting are different from ours. The prophet Isaiah is clear about this: "For my thoughts are not your thoughts, / nor are your ways my ways, says the LORD. / As high as the heavens are above the earth, / so high are my ways above your ways / and my thoughts above your thoughts" (Isaiah 55:8-9). Our deeper mind can appreciate that what is happening is or can be for our own good.

I don't see this. I'm in so much pain that I cannot do anything. I can't even pray. So how is what I am going through helping me?

Despite appearances, be assured that it is. Be as patient as you can with your suffering. Complain if you have to, but hold on as best you can to your faith and trust in God. If your surface mind cannot solve your problem, maybe it will leave the doors open for your deeper mind to come through.

Faith and Constructive Anger

Faith and trust can work with your constructive anger in two ways. Your constructive anger gives you the power to stand and fight or just stand and hold your ground. On the one hand, your faith and trust tell you God is with you. So do not give up. On the other hand, your constructive anger plants you firmly on good solid ground. There your faith and trust can sink their roots and grow.

What are you trying to tell me? I'm not sure what faith and trust and constructive anger and deeper mind means.

Examples of Jesus

Maybe the example of Jesus will help make this clearer.

Because of his faith and trust in his Father, Jesus attempted his mission with confidence. When the Tempter tried to tempt him away from his mission and its hardships by offering the whole world to him if he bowed down and worshiped him, Jesus responded in anger: "Get away, Satan! It is written: / 'The Lord, your God, shall you worship / and him alone shall you serve'" (Matthew 4:10). He said almost the same to Peter when the apostle wanted to spare him pain. "Get behind me, Satan! You are an obstacle to me. You are thinking not as God does, but as human beings do" (Matthew 16:23). In both cases Jesus used his constructive anger to help him keep his faith and trust in God. So his faith and trust helped him use his anger, and his anger helped him keep his faith and trust.

The same was true when Jesus used his deeper mind. On the cross he cries out in pain in the words of Psalm 22:2: "My God, my God, why have you forsaken me?" Despite his pain he continues to believe and trust in his Father, as the rest of the Psalm indicates: "I will proclaim your name to my brethren..../ For he has not spurned nor disdained / the wretched man in his misery" (Psalm 22:23, 25). With his deeper mind he knows his Father will help him. He helped him before when he prayed before Lazarus' tomb. "Father, I thank you for hearing me. I know that you always hear me; but because of the crowd here I have said this, that they may believe that you sent me" (John 11:41-42). So his faith and trust helped him to use his deeper mind, and his deeper mind helped him keep his faith and trust.

Jesus did this often. He combined what he knew from contact with his Father with what he had in the storehouse of his human nature. He is angry, but his anger is filled with faith and trust. He takes the same faith and trust to go into his deeper mind for understanding. With the help of his faith and trust, he cries out in pain, and his cries become a prayer. What makes Jesus so appealing to so many is his use of both sources of help. He has the wisdom and words of God; he has the insights of a deeply committed human.

Profit From Suffering

If you can combine your faith and trust with your constructive anger and deeper mind, you will find a way to profit from your suffering. Like a person lost in a wilderness has contact with the outside world by way of a radio, your faith and trust will keep you in contact with God. Your deeper mind will help you find a path out of the wilderness, and your constructive anger will give you the determination to stay on that path.

I know these sound like hollow words and you are tired of words. You want relief. You feel terrible and you want to feel better. Words are not doing it. You need more.

Jesus felt this same way in his agony in the Garden of Gethsemane. He knew things were going to get a lot worse before they got better. He begged his Father for help. "My Father, if it is possible, let this cup pass from me" (Matthew 26:39). Jesus receives no miracle. He has to hold on with his faith and trust. With his deeper mind he knows that what he is suffering will profit him. With an act of faith and trust, he says, "Not as I will, but as you will." His constructive anger helps him hold on. It helps him to encourage the others to use their anger-determination to rise above the weakness of their flesh.

Your Cross

The words written here do not have to be hollow. You can pick up your cross and carry it or drag it to Calvary. Strangely, mysteriously, your cross can connect you with heaven and earth. Your faith and trust can put you in contact with heaven. Your constructive anger and deeper mind keep you in contact with solid earth. Like Jesus, you can bring together what is heavenly and human.

I have difficulty believing you. Unless I see it for myself, I can't believe any good can come from what I am suffering.

How you feel is understandable. If you can, even if only a little, try to grasp what has been said here. Give it a chance to bring together these different pieces of the puzzle of your life. If it can, the picture that will be formed in you is the picture of Jesus. You will be like him. I would like to tell you about someone who used suffering to do precisely that.

* * *

I met Marie in Long Branch, New Jersey. I was helping with the weekend Masses and stayed on through Monday to give the pastor a day off. Before he left he asked me to visit some of his parishioners in the hospital. It was there that I met Marie. She was in an iron lung and was being treated for an infection.

Marie was thirty when I met her. She had been in the iron lung for fifteen years. I would need the talent of a photographer and the genius of an artist to describe Marie. She was like an act from a magician's show where a woman who is about to be sawed in half has only her head sticking out of the box. That is all Marie presented to those who visited or passed by. With her hair dangling like a waterfall, her twinkling eyes and smile-bright face, she magnetically attracted you. People came from other sections of the hospital to see her. They would go away reassured. If she could smile, they could.

After several visits I got to know Marie quite well. Sickness had ravaged her body. It could not touch her spirit. While her sickness paralyzed her legs and arms and prevented her from walking and swimming, her mind and will were able to take her wherever she wanted to go. She enrolled in television courses given by a nearby college. She listened and learned. Others wrote the answers she dictated to them. She obtained a college degree. When others tried to overdo for her, she would gently remind them that she was an invalid, not a child. Her iron lung had become her second best friend. Jesus was her first.

Marie's physical affliction told her in the clearest terms possible that she was physically handicapped and nothing or little could be done about it. Although the medical profession worked hard to fit her with a portable breathing device, she was too deteriorated to profit from it. On the human, natural level, Marie learned humility. She learned to accept her physical handicap. On the emotional, mental level, she would not let herself be handicapped. These higher parts of her person came through in a supereminent way to make up for her physical deficiencies. On the spiritual level, her love for Jesus taught her to accept her cross out of faith and love. How well she learned to use the natural and supernatural was shown in the invitation I received from her. It read, "I want to invite you to celebrate my twenty-fifth anniversary of doing God's will of being obligated to live in an iron lung. May God be praised!"

I welled up with pride as I read the invitation because I had learned to love the heart that wrote it. She was so excited on one visit because she could not wait to tell me that she had fallen in love with a doctor. I was excited to hear it.

A few years ago I received a note from her mother that Marie had died. I was sad and glad. I was sad because Marie is not with us to be a light shining in the dark. I was glad because she has been released from her imprisonment, and I was ever so grateful to God for showing me once again how much beauty could exist in the midst of great suffering.

* * *

1. Does it make sense that although Jesus and nature approach suffering differently, they are not opposed to each other?
2. Do you know how to convert your fear into constructive anger?
3. Do you believe you have a *deeper* mind?
4. Do you see how your faith and trust in God can help you use your constructive anger and deeper mind? Do you see how your constructive anger and deeper mind can be a support to your faith and trust in God?

5

Facing the Mystery of Evil

People react to the sufferings of life in many different ways. Some are crushed by what happens to them. Bitterness permeates their entire being. In their desperate efforts to achieve some relief, they turn on others, even on those who are trying to help them. Frequently, they turn on God. Why is he allowing this? We, who are not in their situation, have no right to condemn them and we don't — nor does God. But it's clear that their pain and misery have overcome them. They are defeated and broken people.

This isn't surprising considering the severity of their sufferings, but fortunately, that's not the whole story. There are other people who react differently to this same experience. In fact, with them just the opposite happens. Somehow they are ennobled by their sufferings. Perhaps you have met some of these good people. Throughout their lives everything bad happens to them, not once but time and again. The afflictions they experience are as harsh as those dealt to the first group. Yet somehow these individuals rise above it all. When you meet them, you know they are suffering as much as anyone else, yet there are no curses on their lips — only words of praise and thanksgiving. How do they do it?

Yes, that's what I'd like to know. Thank you for reminding me of them. I have indeed met such inspiring people myself. How impressed I was! But in my own pain, in what I have been going through lately, I had forgotten about them. How do they do it? What is their secret?

The Secret

Yes, what is their secret? That's what we've been trying to discover. The psychiatrist Viktor Frankl would say that they had discovered a meaning for their sufferings. That the terrible experiences they were going through were not absurd and meaningless. He would quote the philosopher Friedrich Nietzsche: "He who has a *why* to live for can bear almost any *how.*"

Dr. Frankl spoke from experience. He had survived three years at Auschwitz and other Nazi concentration camps. Once he was free, he reestablished his clinical practice. One day a gentleman came to him who was terribly depressed. His wife had died two years before. He missed her so much that his grief continued to overwhelm him. Dr. Frankl asked him to suppose that he, rather than his wife, had died first. What about that? The man answered that his death would have been terrible for her, that she would have suffered greatly. The doctor reminded him that he had spared his wife this great suffering, but now he had to pay for this loving act by surviving and mourning her. On hearing these words, the depression left him. His suffering continued but now it was different. It had a meaning.

This is helping me grasp a little better what you said earlier. You said that God has an overall plan that includes the particular suffering I'm going through. He can see the whole picture and oftentimes I don't. It's good to be reminded of that.

Yes, that's right. Your suffering is certainly not meaningless. Even though you might not fully understand what the meaning is or how it fits into the whole picture, you can be sure of one thing: this plan is wise and loving since it comes from God.

Though I'm doing better, I have to admit I'm still having a problem with that. You said that God's plan was wise and loving; you also said that suffering happened to good people. I have trouble putting these two concepts together. Why does God let good people, even innocent people, suffer?

The Mystery of Evil

This, of course, is part of that very big question: if God is good and all-powerful, why does he allow evil in the world? From the very beginning, human beings have been asking that question. Philosophers, theologians, the greatest thinkers the world has known, have struggled with this problem, the great mystery of evil. We are grateful for the answers we have heard, even though they have been only partial answers, little snatches of the truth.

Some have pointed out that much of the evil in our world has been the result of human actions. This is easy to verify. Scanning the newspaper or tuning in to the evening news provides a running account of the wars, murders, mayhem, and cruelties that human beings inflict upon one another every day. Not to mention prejudice, racism, the destruction of the environment, corruption in high places, assorted injustices. And we shouldn't forget the involvement with evil by the individual, what we do to ourselves by abusing food and drink, by carelessness about our health, by self-centeredness, and by lack of commitment in our relationships.

In a way some people have tried to blame God for these expressions of evil in our world. Their argument is that if God had not given free will to human beings then these terrible things would not have happened. That's correct: if there's no free will then there's no sin, no personal evil. But, remember, that means there wouldn't be any possibility of genuine love either. To have the ability *to love* means you must also have the ability *not to love,* that is, the ability to sin. Jesus tells the story of the farmer who sowed good seed in his field. Then his enemy came and sowed weeds among the wheat. God's creation was good, but by the bad use of our free will, we became evil and corrupted our creation. We brought in evil and suffering. It is our fault, not God's.

But what about physical evils that are not caused by human beings? What about hurricanes, tornadoes, floods, droughts, and other natural disasters? Also all those terrible sicknesses like cancer, multiple sclerosis, emphysema, cerebral palsy, heart attacks, plagues, AIDS, mental and emotional illnesses — the list is practically endless — what about those evils? If God's plan is so wise and loving, why are these included in it?

The World Is Incomplete

One answer is that when God made the world, he made it incomplete. He deliberately didn't finish it so we could have a hand in completing it. This would make it our world as well as his. We would be cocreators with him in helping the world reach its destiny.

Slow down. Are you saying God planned an incomplete world on purpose so we could help him complete it? That doesn't sound very wise. It doesn't seem like it would justify all the suffering that's in the world. Moreover, what can I complete? I can barely handle my sufferings, how can I complete the world?

You help God complete his creation when you use your intelligence and help God work the raw materials into finished products. When you plant a seed and help it grow, you are helping to complete creation. When you raise a child to arrive at full physical, emotional, and rational maturity, you are helping to complete creation. There are a thousand ways to do this. Every advancement of science and medicine, every enrichment of knowledge, every suffering endured, and every loving act performed help to complete this world that is both God's and yours.

I still don't see how my actions could have any effect on this world I'm living in. I especially don't understand how my suffer-ings could help complete the world. Can you explain further?

The Sufferings of Jesus

There is no doubt that we are dealing with a mystery here. In his letter to the Christian community at Colossae, Saint Paul has a statement about suffering that is somewhat puzzling. Even so, it might point us in the right direction. He says: "Now I rejoice in my sufferings for your sake, and in my flesh I am filling up what is lacking in the afflictions of Christ" (Colossians 1:24).

That phrase, *what is lacking,* is variously interpreted by the scholars. It does not imply that Christ's atoning death on the cross was defective in any way. Some see it as saying that the Church, as the Mystical Body of Christ, will have a quota of "woes" to be endured before the end of the world. Other scholars suggest that Saint Paul's total dedication to Christ, his ability to unite himself with the Lord, allowed him to call his own sufferings the "afflic-tions of Christ." In either interpretation the tie-in with Jesus' sufferings is apparent. The good news is that what Saint Paul believed about his sufferings is also applicable to what you are experiencing. Your sufferings are linked to Christ's. You may not understand *how* but you don't have to. You can leave that up to God. The least you can say is that your sufferings are certainly not meaningless. Rather, they are priceless because of their intimate connection with our Savior's.

You have given me a lot of things to think about. I'm sure I don't understand everything that was said. But let's see if I have some of these ideas straight. God has a wise and loving plan for me, which includes my sufferings. They are not without meaning, even when I don't understand what's happening or why. God made an incomplete creation. Good people, including innocent children, are part of this incomplete creation, and that's why suffering can come to them, even though they don't deserve it. Part of our job on earth, one of the reasons we are here, is to complete God's creation, to make it a better world. We can do this by using our talents, by doing good things, and even by suffering. One of the reasons my sufferings can do this is because they can be joined to Christ's. I don't understand how this works, but I feel that I have come across a truth here that I would like to know more about.

You have understood a lot. Remember, we are dealing with some very big mysteries here. The first one is the mystery of evil. I mentioned that the great minds of the world have wrestled with this one. Why is there evil in the world? Tied in with that is the mystery of free will. There's also the mystery of completing creation and your role in this. Finally, there is the great mystery of God himself and his loving plan for you.

Would you say more about that? Maybe that's what I need. I still feel upset and shaky. I think my mind has more or less accepted what you've said, but my feelings aren't going along with it yet. I guess I still feel alone and helpless. Does God really care about me?

God's Providence

Perhaps this will help. One of the terms for God's loving plan is providence. Providence means to see ahead. It is the same as the word *provide*. One who provides sees ahead to what is needed. This is what God has done. He has seen ahead and provided for all your needs. He has done this several ways.

Before you were a twinkle in your parents' eyes, God had a loving plan ready for you. At your conception God packed into your beginnings everything you would ever need to cope and grow — physically, emotionally, and spiritually. It took time and work to unpack each level of your being. The physical was the easiest to open. The emotional and spiritual needed much more work before they opened. These are the natural resources God has provided for you.

Second, above and beyond these natural resources, God foresaw and placed special people and circumstances in your life to help you cope and grow. They might not have seemed special at the time, but when you look back, you see they were.

Third, you were given Jesus' offer of help.

I think you are coming closer to something I need. I need to know God is watching over me and not letting me out of his sight. I need to know he has not forgotten me. I need to know he is helping me. I need to know he cares. I need reassurance that he is allowing what is happening because good will come from it. Can you go deeper into this providence God has for me?

God's Care for You

Yes, there is a great amount that can be said about this close-at-hand help God gives you. God has a super vision over you. That means he sees or has a vision of all the details of your life in a super way. He arranges them for your good. As Saint Paul says, "We know that all things work for good for those who love God" (Romans 8:28). Jesus, referring to what is necessary for life and growth, says, "Your heavenly Father knows that you need them all" (Matthew 6:32). Jesus also says that if God helps the birds and flowers, how much more will he help you. (See Luke 12:22-28.) So you can count on God's help. Trust him. Feel his nearness.

As I've said before, I used to count on God's help. Since I've gotten sick and he hasn't helped me, I'm not sure anymore. Sometimes I feel he must hate me and that is why he is not helping me. Does he?

Of course not. He does not hate you. He loves you. He will not forget you. As God says through Isaiah in the Old Testament: "Can a mother forget her infant, / be without tenderness for the child of her womb? / Even should she forget, / I will never forget you. / See, upon the palms of my hands I have written your name" (Isaiah 49:15-16).

God has not forgotten you. The following story tells about another person who also wondered if God loved him.

* * *

John was a good man. He was always helping people. On weekends he would help at the church. His wife and family understood and approved of what he was doing. He was sensitive to their needs, so they did not feel rejected or ignored.

A good part of John's inner life had been a struggle trying to sort things out. So often he felt empty and didn't know why. Maybe that was why he was always busy. It kept his mind on others and not on himself.

One day in his early sixties, John was busy setting up booths for his church's annual bazaar. All was going well until he slipped on some oil someone had spilled. He fell down on his side with a cracking sound. The things he was carrying went flying. On the ground in pain, John tried to make light of what had happened. He laughed nervously, but the pain told him that this was not a laughing matter. He tried to get up, but he could not. A couple of men nearby tried to help him up, but he begged them to stop. One of the men went for help. The EMS unit came quickly. One look told them John had broken his hip.

As John lay in the hospital bed after his family left for the evening, he went back over what had happened. Why had he not seen the oil spot? Why had someone not done something about the oil spill? Why had God allowed this to happen? Was this the way to repay him for doing good? It wasn't fair. It wasn't even smart. So few today go out of their way to help others. Now there would be one less. These and other questions haunted John's mind as he lay in bed, helpless.

Not wanting to be a crybaby, John kept these questions to himself. He didn't even bring them up to the chaplain who visited him daily. But one day it was the chaplain who gave him the opening. "John," he said, "people in your condition often have difficulties in trying to understand what has happened to them. Once the shock wears off they begin to ask all kinds of questions about life, God, and other things. Has this happened to you?"

"Father, now that you've asked, I'll be honest. I have a lot of questions. I can't understand why this happened to me. I go to Mass and Communion weekly. I help everyone I can. I don't hurt or burden anyone, so why am I here? Why didn't God help me? What is the sense of praying and being good if God is not going to help me?"

"John," the chaplain answered, "I'm glad you are asking these questions. They are good ones. Maybe they can lead to some better ones. Did God see my need to slow down? Did he see that I am missing out on deeper dimensions of life? Is God trying to teach me something of value for this life and for eternal life where he can make up for any unfairness he allows in this life?"

John did not know what to answer. He felt very small. Of course, there had to be good reasons why God allowed what happened to him. He would not be God if there were none. He thanked the priest for listening and opening some windows that could let some light into his mind. He asked the priest for his blessing.

* * *

1. Do you wonder at times why God did not do a better job of creating? Why does God allow so much evil in this world?
2. Can you see anything good that can come from suffering?
3. Do you find the suffering of good people a stumbling block in approaching God? Why do the innocent suffer? Why does anyone suffer?
4. Can you discover any meaning in your own suffering?
5. What is God's providence? How does God see ahead and provide for all your needs?

6

Discovering Peace Despite Pain

Perhaps the most difficult thing about suffering is not the pain you experience but the fear it breeds.

Pain is pain. No one likes it. Most of the time it is looked on as an evil to be avoided and rightly so. That's a normal reaction to suffering of any kind. Avoid it. Do what you can to rid your life of pain.

Pain and Fear

Sometimes it seems that the worst part of pain is not the pain itself but the fear that surrounds it. Once fear starts to work on a person's imagination, it can intensify the pain and make it almost unbearable. If uncontrolled, fear can almost scare a person to death. So if you can lessen your fear, you may also alleviate your pain to the same extent.

I know what you are saying. It probably is fear that is making my pain worse. But what am I supposed to do? I don't know how to handle my fears. Can you help me?

It's not an easy problem to solve. We have to take it apart and answer it a piece at a time.

47

You have been given the emotion of fear for the same reason you were given pain sensors in your body. Thus, in this case, as with pain, fear is meant to help you. Fear alerts you to danger. Fear informs you that something might harm you, so you had better get ready for it. Fear prepares you to either fight or run. So fear is designed as a protective device. But it can get out of hand. When that happens it makes everything worse, including your pain.

I know that, but what can I do about it? I can't handle fear. As soon as it strikes, I panic. I'm not proud of myself but that's the truth. I don't know what to do with my fear.

The Power of Hope

Maybe the following truths can help you. Besides constructive anger, God has placed inside of you a virtue or power we call hope. You have convinced yourself that you cannot handle fear. Your attitude has become a habit. You need to reverse the habit. Instead of saying, "I can't do it. I can't do it," you need to say, "I hope I can do it. I hope I can do it." Your constructive anger would say, "I'm going to do it. I'm going to do it." If you cannot tap your anger-strength, maybe you can tap your hope-strength and say, "I hope I can do it." That can help in several ways.

If you are in depression, hope can help relieve that. Depression is a state of being hopeless. If you are isolated in your pain, hope can assure you that you are not alone. If you are in darkness, hope can provide at least a glimmer of light.

I don't think this is going to help. I can say the words, but they will be like a whisper telling a strong wind to calm down. No, I don't think saying "I hope I can do it" will help. I don't have it within me.

No, you don't, but you are not alone.

Fortunately, you have the power of God behind you and your words. If there is one thing that is not lacking in the Scriptures, it is words of encouragement, words of hope. From the Book of

Genesis to the Book of Revelation, the pages of the Bible proclaim hope in season and out. The constant theme is that God is with you. Do not despair. Christ expresses it well when he says, "Do not let your hearts be troubled. You have faith in God; have faith also in me" (John 14:1). What he is saying is "trust me. Hope in me." He chides those who are in difficult situations and do not trust him. (See Matthew 8:26.)

So you have God's power behind your words. What you need most of all is you behind your words. Do not let your fears overwhelm you. You are more than your fears. You are you. Your fears are only a part of you.

If you can believe that God is true to his word and that God has placed special powers inside of you for coping with a crisis, you have a basis for hope. Help is available. To get you in contact with it, you have to make some sparks, some sparks of hope.

But how?

Sparks of fire are made by rubbing hard objects together — flint against flint or wood against stone. You have two hard objects you are dealing with. You have the seemingly impossible situation you are in and the rocks of fear and despair inside of you. Rub them together. Get angry with your situation. Get angry with yourself for tiring of God's help and providence. Get a fire going, the fire of hope. Keep telling yourself, "I hope. I hope. I trust. I trust."

That's not going to work. I don't feel like I trust God. I know I don't trust myself. I feel like I have no hope. I'm completely hopeless.

You may feel that way but you are not. People in worse situations have found ways to hope. So can you. If you cannot reach into yourself for help, reach out to others. Above all, reach out to God. You may feel he does not care because he has not been helping you, but he does.

If you can develop some hope, you can cancel the intensity of your fear. If your fear lets up, your mind can let up on the worry that has been devastating you. Once that eases, you will have some peace. Your task, then, is to work on hope.

How?

To start with, it's all right to hope that your sickness and your pain can be fixed by medical practice or by a miracle. If it turns out that the miracle does not occur, hope that you will grow stronger in other parts of your personality, in your emotions and your faith and trust in God. If these grow stronger, you will be able to handle the weight of your burden, no matter how heavy it is. What you cannot handle, God will. In either case, you can be at peace.

Peace — what I would not give to be at peace. Is it really possible to find peace even in the midst of suffering?

Yes, it is. To arrive at it, you must put things in order. What you can handle by developing your hope and constructive anger, handle. What you cannot handle, hope that God will.

In seeking peace, it's good to realize there are two approaches you can use. The more common approach to peace is to be freed of worries or fear. This is the one most people seek.

The Way of Positives

A second, stronger approach to peace is by way of positives. The positive elements in your life can outweigh the negatives; the good can outweigh the bad. If you have something good happening in your life, you can be at peace even though bad things are also happening. The good is stronger than the bad. For example, if you really love someone deeply, you can override pain and misfortune. You are so buoyed up by the positive effects of your deep loving that you consider the negatives as of lesser account. You are at peace because your love is so deep and fulfilling.

But what if you do not have any positives, what then? What if you have no one to love? All I have is misery. I have no positives. I do not have my health or any real friends I can count on. Where do I go to find these positives that bring peace?

These are not easy questions to answer. If you are overshadowed by the darkness of negatives, it's difficult to see any light, anywhere. Still, there is a light for you. God has provided one for you. Where is it? If it's not from humans, it can be from God himself. It can be from Jesus. He says of himself, "I am the light of the world. Whoever follows me will not walk in darkness, but will have the light of life" (John 8:12). Why not turn to Jesus? Why not turn your life over to him?

I would like to but I don't know how.

You do it by doing it. Tell him simply, "Jesus, I'm turning my life over to you. I don't understand what's happening to me. I don't understand why you have not helped me. God knows I've prayed and others have prayed for me. I give my life to you. It's yours. Take it. If you want me to accomplish something in this life, help me. If not, your will be done. I trust you. I hope in you. I know I won't be disappointed."

With such a prayer, you cannot fail. You are opening doors of love inside of you for the Divine to enter. You are accepting the highest challenge in life — to trust Jesus, to trust that God is a good Father.

Jesus – Your Peace

So Jesus can be your peace. The Letter to the Ephesians says, "For he is our peace" (2:14). He is ready to do more. He is ready to accept you with open arms. That is why he stretched them out on the cross — to welcome you. Bring your own pain-ridden body to him. He knows what pain is. He knows what abandonment feels like.

I don't know if I can do what you suggest. I can try. Is that good enough?

It is.

In the story that follows, trying was good enough for Joelle also.

* * *

Successful in her professional career and happily married, Joelle was in her mid forties when she realized how big the bigness of life can be. She began to walk through doors inside of her that she never knew existed. They were the doors of deepest love.

Joelle had read the Bible several times. She liked the Bible because it was filled with accounts about people and what they had done with their lives. Although of a different time, they were real and came alive as she read. God was real and alive too. But when she closed the Bible, it was like when she was a child and put her dolls away after playing with them. They went to sleep and she went on with her life. She did the same with the Bible. She closed its covers and it had little effect on her life.

Things changed for Joelle after her sixth child. The child was prematurely born and brain damaged. She felt so bad — for herself, her family, and the baby. All kinds of questions ran through her head. Why couldn't she be content the way things were? Why did she have another child? Why did God allow this to happen? Was she being punished like people she read about in the Bible? If so, for what? The questions tired her out, but they kept coming and coming.

Not knowing where to turn for answers, Joelle picked up her Bible. She turned to the New Testament. Her eyes fell on the passages where Joseph and Mary presented Jesus to God. "When the days were completed for their purification according to the law of Moses, they took him up to Jerusalem to present him to the Lord....Now there was a man in Jerusalem whose name was Simeon....Simeon blessed them and said to Mary his mother, 'Behold, this child is destined for the fall and rise of many in Israel, and to be a sign that will be contradicted (and you yourself a sword will pierce) so that the thoughts of many hearts may be revealed" (Luke 2:22, 25, 34-35).

"My God," Joelle exclaimed, "these words apply to me and my

child. He is being crucified by his brain-damaged condition and my soul is being torn apart by doubts so it can expand and find room for this crucified child."

Something happened in Joelle. A light was coming through the dark of her darkness and a calm settled over her. Like Joseph, she heard inside of her, "Do not be afraid, Joelle, to take on the care of this child for he is from God. He will teach you the deepest kind of love." (See Matthew 1:20-22.) Almost repeating Mary's words, Joelle said, "I am a child of God. Let it be as my Father has chosen to let it happen." (See Luke 1:38.)

She called the child Christian.

* * *

1. When you are in pain, what is worse, the pain itself or the fear it causes?
2. How do you react to fear? What can you do to lessen or relieve fear?
3. What is hope? Have you lost your trust in God? Can God be God and be untrue to his promises to help you? Does he not have to help you, since he promised so many times in the Bible he would?
4. Does being at peace mean you are freed of worries or fears? Are there any positives in your life? If you do not find positives in human relationships, can you find some in your relationship with God? Can you let Jesus be your peace?

7

Accepting the Challenges of Life and Love

Although this topic of suffering is so big and mysterious that not a thousand books would ever be able to enter all its paths, I want to bring this book to a close by considering the challenges suffering offers us. Much of this concluding chapter will simply sum up what has been touched on in the other chapters.

Invitation to a Banquet

At what seems to be the worst time of your life, suffering invites you to a banquet of life and love. It is a banquet where many are called but few accept the invitation. (See Matthew 22:1-14.) Why? Mostly because they do not understand it. They are afraid of pain. It blocks the doorway to this banquet. That is unfortunate. For a few moments, go beyond this doorway of pain into the banquet hall. See what is being offered.

Suffering is an invitation to the fullness of life. Only when all the parts of our being are fulfilled or in the process of being fulfilled is pain absent. Only then does the fullness of peace settle in and reassure us that our life is as it should be. If this fullness of peace is not present, then something is lacking somewhere in our personality. It could be lacking in our physical being. Something is broken or incomplete. It could be lacking in our emotional being. Our emotions are in conflict with one another or are striving to become unblocked. It could be lacking in our spiritual being. When we should have clear directions, we are wandering around aimlessly and lost. The pain we experience is there to help us. It is like a red flag warning us that something needs our immediate attention.

I think I understand what you are saying, but I'm not sure. I have spent so many years of my life looking on pain or suffering as a punishment, as something to be avoided at all costs, that I'm having trouble getting a different viewpoint. I know you have attempted throughout this book to change my way of thinking. If you could throw a little more light on the ways suffering offers a fullness of life, it might help.

The Process of Maturing

For a deeper understanding of the purpose of pain, it's important to stand back and consider a very obvious, important fact of our life here on earth. The fact is that we are continuously in the process of maturing. As with vegetables and fruits, the flowers are not enough. As beautiful as they might be, they are only the beginning of the life of the vegetable or fruit. They must bear the heat of the summer, the whipping winds, and the watering rains. If they do not, their beginning promises of life will never reach fulfillment.

We are like them. In the beginning most of us are protected from the more serious aspects of our personality development. Our flesh is young. Our bodies are strong. Our emotions are simple. Our minds are clear. There are falls and bruises, but they are quickly healed. The tears have hardly dried and we are off and running.

Then a different awareness of life begins. How? It differs for each of us. It could be that sickness or death visits our family or neighborhood. That scares us. It could be that the people who have protected us are scared over some aspect of life. Their fears infect us with fears.

There are so many ways that we can be awakened or be shaken from our innocence about life. Once that happens, what will we do? Will we close our eyes and pretend that ugly things do not exist? Will we turn to God and ask him to protect us against the challenges of life?

Whatever we do, whatever God does, the challenges of life are real. They are necessary if we are to grow to maturity. Most often it is pain that awakens us from our innocence. Is that good? Is that bad? Evidently, it could be good or God would not allow it. In the long run, what makes it good is if we understand the purpose of pain and accept its challenges of life. They are the challenges of fulfillment. They are the challenges of love.

Love's Challenges

The main purpose for arriving at personal fulfillment is love.

When we love, we want to give our fullness to the other. We want to offer him or her a full, even overflowing, cup of ourselves. How much the other can drink or will accept our offering depends on that person's development. With regard to God, obviously he can and will accept whatever we can offer him. Look at the overflowing fullness Jesus offers us on the cross. He could not stretch his arms out any further to embrace us. Painful as it is, he even has them nailed to the cross, so if they tire, they will not fall. They are always open to us.

Maybe what you are saying will help me to accept my pain as something more than something to be endured. Expand on pain as an invitation to a banquet of love.

Pain is an invitation to love in as much as it is an invitation to fulfillment. It lets us know the places or parts within us that are empty because they are cracked, blocked, or incomplete. Once these parts are repaired, love can enter them more freely. So pain is an invitation to the banquet of love. Answering the needs pain points out is our positive response to attend and fully participate.

But isn't a willingness to suffer also a response to love? It seems to me if I offer my pain to God that should tell him how much I love him. Am I wrong?

No, you are not wrong. When you offer your pain, what you are really offering God is your faith and trust in him. You are telling him that you love and trust him even though you do not understand why he is not helping you, why the pain continues.

Does it matter if I don't understand all of this and just offer God my pain?

No, it doesn't matter. What matters is what is in your heart. God sees your love.

So, no matter how you understand it, your pain is an invitation to love. Try to accept this invitation with a positive response. "Yes, God, reserve a seat for me in your banquet of love. I'll do my best to attend."

The Eternal Banquet

These banquets of life and love that pain invites you to are rehearsals of the eternal banquet. Now, in this life, you experience so much more of life and love when you understand the purpose of pain. Later, in eternal life, you will experience the feast of life and love in their utmost fullness. As Saint Paul says, "For this momentary light affliction is producing for us an eternal weight of glory beyond all comparison" (2 Corinthians 4:17).

Besides these treasures of eternal life, you will find answers to your deepest complaints. Many complain that life is not fair. Because God does not prevent the sufferings of good and innocent people, many conclude that he is unfair. From the human viewpoint it may seem that way. But God has an eternity to make up to you for any unfair treatment you have received. God is not stingy. He will not be outdone in generosity. "There is no one who has given up house or brothers or sisters or mother or father or children or lands for my sake and for the sake of the gospel who will not receive a hundred times more now in this present age…and eternal life in the age to come" (Mark 10:29-30). Surely, God will repay any present unfairness in ways beyond your imagining.

Who can adequately imagine what the banquet of eternal life and love are like? Perhaps the one who can come closest is the one who loves deeply. He or she leaves self and goes so deeply into the other that the other is not another but is the person loving. Such a oneness takes place that the two are not just one body but they are one being. One is hardly distinguishable from the other. They flow together like two rivers. This leaving of themselves is what an ecstasy is all about. The ecstasy of the eternal banquet is this and so much more. With Saint Paul we can exclaim:

"What eye has not seen, and ear has not heard,
    and what has not entered the human heart,
    what God has prepared for those who love him."

(1 Corinthians 2:9)

Saint Paul knew from some of his personal experiences what the eternal banquet must be like. "I know someone in Christ who…was caught up into Paradise and heard ineffable things, which no one may utter" (2 Corinthians 12:2, 4).

Be at Peace

Be at peace as much as you can. Under the tossing wind and waves, down deep inside of you, be at peace. The kingdom is yours. Jesus has won it for you. Bear what you are suffering with hope. It seems like your suffering will never end, but it will. The kingdom of eternal life and love will not. With your hand hold on to your rosary or crucifix. With your mind hold on to the promises of Jesus. With your heart hold on to hope. Wait with hope for those rewarding words of Christ, "Well done, my good and faithful servant. Since you were faithful in small matters, I will give you great responsibilities. Come, share your master's joy" (Matthew 25:21).

The following story is about getting ready for the heavenly banquet.

* * *

Jean and her daughter Terry were inseparable. Even when they were away, they were together.

One day at work, Terry felt so dizzy she thought she would faint. Her girlfriend took her home. At home she felt a little better. "It's only because I have been working too hard," she told herself. "I'll feel better in the morning."

But she did not feel better. She felt worse. After calling in sick at work, she went to a doctor who gave her a thorough exam. As gently as he could, he told her he suspected the presence of a brain tumor. He sent her to a specialist for more tests. His suspicions were correct.

When Jean was told of Terry's condition, she could hardly believe what was happening. At first she begged God for a miracle. As Terry got worse, Jean threatened God that if he did such an unnatural thing as to take a daughter before the mother, she would end her relationship with him.

Three months from her first dizzy spell, Terry died.

Although technically alive, Jean died too. As her sons carried her to her seat in the church for the funeral service, she screamed, "He lies. He lies. Jesus said, 'If you ask anything in my name, I will give it to you.' I asked. I begged, and he did nothing, absolutely nothing. He lies. He lies."

Months later Jean haunted the church. She didn't want to be there, but there was no other place to go. Ever since she was a child, she had attended daily Mass. One morning after Mass, she stopped me and asked why God did not answer her prayers. "He did," I answered. "You asked for more life for Terry and God has given it to her. I attended Terry before she died, and she was radiant with the thought of going to God. For the first time in her life, she was not afraid to die. Believe me, she was truly happy."

"She could not be happy," Jean shouted bitterly. "She wanted to live. I needed her to live."

I said nothing. I knew Jean's words were bursting from a wounded heart. It would, hopefully, heal with time. I took her hand and lifted her from the bench. I held her until her body stopped trembling.

On another occasion Jean stopped me and asked, "Why doesn't God take me? I don't want to live."

I said to her, gently, "He will. In the meantime, you have work to do. Terry was a very loving person. I was the recipient of her love and generosity many times, but her love was very emotional. It needs deepening. She is probably involved in that deepening process now and needs help. Your prayers and acts of love and trust in God can help her. We know that our love and prayers help those in that deepening state called purgatory. So your work as a mother is not over. When it is, God will take you."

Jean was stunned away from her grief and from feeling sorry for herself. She didn't fully understand what I was saying, but if what she understood was true that her love and life could help Terry, she would do what she could to be patient with God and the terrible ache in her heart. She forced herself to say, "Your will be done."

* * *

1. Can you see that suffering is an invitation to a banquet? Can you see that it is like the banquet Jesus speaks about in the gospels? Will you respond to it by using your suffering to expand your life and love?

2. Would you rather have God challenge your life to its highest growth or leave you alone where you are in your development? Can you see that suffering is such a challenge and that is the only reason God allows it?
3. Have you ever loved from a deep fulfillment or has your love been mostly from need? Has anyone ever loved you from a deep fulfillment or has it always been from need?
4. What does eternal life mean to you? Is it the absence of pain and the fullness of pleasures? Is it the fulfillment of love and joy? Is it worth the admission price of the challenges of suffering?

Conclusion

In conclusion, I want to tell you that my brother died. The cruel cancer that invaded him would not let up. Neither the medical profession nor prayers could stop it. It was a grueling struggle for him and the family. Now it's over. He has gone to God. He has gone home.

So the words of this book will not be for him and his encouragement but, hopefully, they can be of some help to others. Selfishly, I hope they will be a help to me when I might need them. I know from personal experience the devastating effects of weakness and fear. When you are not yourself, the self you are used to, everything changes. Life becomes a fear. Mortality becomes a monster ready to devour you at any moment. Imagination becomes a runaway horse. You don't know where it will go with your fear. Others can help. They can be a source of strength with their love, sympathy, encouragement, and physical assistance. Unfortunately, they cannot stop your slide into helplessness.

Only God and a deep awareness that what you are suffering is not in vain can help. Your faith and trust can be a net to catch your fall. They are your hope and security. With them, somewhere inside, you know you will be all right. You will not feel great, but you know you are in strong hands. They will not let go of you until they help you over the walls of this life to eternal life. You can count on that. Amen.

Some Acts of Faith
for Someone Suffering

Jesus, I believe you are a king.

I believe you are the king of everyone — those who know you and those who do not.

I believe you want to be known as a king of the afflicted.

I believe you are the Suffering Servant the Old Testament speaks of.

I believe you will judge us on the last day on the basis of our concern for the hungry, the thirsty, the stranger, the naked, the sick, the imprisoned. (See Matthew 25:31-40.)

I believe you are like your Father who promised to rescue his sheep who are scattered when it is cloudy and dark, who are lost, injured, and sick. (See Ezekiel 34:11-12, 15-17.)

I believe you can help me in these hours of my life that are so cloudy and dark that I am almost hopeless.

Jesus, I believe in you.

A Prayer

Dear Jesus, I come to you sick, naked of health, imprisoned in fear. Please help me. I know you can. Help me to have the kind of faith that works miracles. I believed in you as a child when I did not know how difficult life could be. Now that I know, I have become a child again needing to take someone's hand. Jesus, into your hands I place my life. Please help me. Please remove this cross that is weighing me down. Please make me feel your helping presence. Please help me to accept that the only reason you might not be answering my prayers the way I want you to is because you know what is best for me — for time, for eternity. Because you know what I do not know, I will pray as you prayed in the Garden, "Not my will be done but yours." Amen.

The Price of Admission

"When the strong fall, what hope is there for the weak?"
Thus reasons the unthinking man.
"Oh," God sighed, not knowing what else to do,
"Have I been with you so long and you do not understand?

"It is in your weakness that my strength is revealed,
It is when you are sick that you come to me to be healed.

"It was from the fabric of nothingness, I created each star.
It was from nothingness, I formed the masterpiece you are.

"If weakness teaches you this — that to me you belong —
Then your weakness has not made you weak, it has made you strong.

"So come to me and I will give you my strength.
More than this, I will give you life without length.

"I will give you the keys opening beyond the doors of strife,
I will welcome you into the banquet of everlasting life."